ZOO ANIMALS
IN THE WILD

SNAKE

JINNY JOHNSON

ILLUSTRATED BY GRAHAM ROSEWARNE

A⁺

Smart Apple Media

Published by Smart Apple Media

2140 Howard Drive West, North Mankato, Minnesota 56003

Designed by Helen James
Illustrated by Graham Rosewarne

Photographs by Robert E. Barber, Corbis (Anthony Bannister; Gallo Images,
Annie Griffiths Belt, Michael & Patricia Fogden, Frank Lane Picture Agency, Stephen
Frink, COLLART HERVE/CORBIS SYGMA, Linda Lewis; Frank Lane Picture Agency,
Chris Mattison; Frank Lane Picture Agency, Joe McDonald, Mary Ann McDonald,
David A. Northcott, Rob C. Nunnington; Gallo Images, Rod Patterson; Gallo Images,
Jeffery L. Rotman, Kevin Schafer, Alastair Shay; Papilio)

Printed and bound in Thailand

Library of Congress Cataloging-in-Publication Data

Johnson, Jinny.
Snake / by Jinny Johnson.
p. cm. — (Zoo animals in the wild)
ISBN 1-58340-644-1
1. Snakes—Juvenile literature. I. Title.

QL666.O6J638 2005
597.96—dc22   2004062550

First Edition

9 8 7 6 5 4 3 2 1

Contents

Snakes

Snakes are amazing creatures that manage to live in most parts of the world. Most snakes live in warm places, but some snakes live high on mountains or even in the ocean.

A snake has a long body that ends in a pointed tail, but it has no legs or arms. Its body is not slimy. It is covered with tough, dry scales that overlap each other like the shingles on a roof. The scales help to protect the snake's body from heat and damage.

A common adder warms itself in the sun.

A snake's body is covered with colorful scales.

Snakes are cold-blooded animals, which means that they can't make their own body heat. Instead, snakes lie in the sun to warm themselves and crawl into the shade to cool down.

An Australian sea snake searches for food underwater.

Kinds of snakes

There are about 2,700 different kinds of snakes. Some of the best-known are pythons, boas, cobras, and rattlesnakes. The smallest snakes are only the size of an adult's pinky finger. The longest snake is the reticulated python, which is longer than five tall adults lying head to toe.

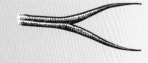

The vine snake is one of the thinnest of all snakes.

Many different kinds of snakes are kept in zoos—even some of the biggest, such as the reticulated python and the anaconda.

A yellow anaconda rests in its zoo home.

A snake's skeleton is made up mostly of its backbone and ribs. Humans have only 12 pairs of ribs. Many snakes have more than 200 pairs of ribs, which help keep their body strong yet flexible.

The reticulated python is so big that it can hunt animals as large as pigs.

At home in the wild

Snakes live in steamy jungles, sandy deserts, and dry, rocky areas. Many climb trees and curl their long body around the branches. Others hide in holes or cracks in rocks, and a few find shelter in underground burrows.

Many snakes like water. The anaconda spends most of its life in rivers and moves faster in water than on land.

The horned viper lives in the desert sands of Africa.

Some snakes move around to find food during the day, but others come out only at night. Snakes spend much of their time resting between meals.

A snake's skin gets worn and damaged as it moves. Several times a year, a snake molts, or sheds its outer skin.

A Malagasy cat-eye tree snake.

Like other snakes, a rat snake sheds its skin all at once.

9

At home in the zoo

A snake's home in the zoo doesn't need to be very big, but it should be about the same temperature as its home in the wild. The enclosure needs to be at least two-thirds the length of the snake's body and contain some rocks or branches for the snake to slither on.

Most snake enclosures have glass fronts so visitors can look at the snakes safely.

A monocled cobra at the Denver Zoo.

A zoo snake also needs something rough to rub against when it's time to shed its skin.

All zoo snakes need some water in their home. Many snakes like to have a pool large enough to swim or soak in.

An anaconda enjoys a dip in the pool in its enclosure.

11

Finding food

All snakes catch and eat other creatures. Some snakes actively hunt for their food. Others simply lie in wait for their prey. They stay hidden until an animal such as a lizard, frog, or worm comes near, then dart forward to seize it in their jaws.

Snakes cannot chew, so they must swallow their food whole.

Boas and pythons eat animals such as mice, rats, and rabbits. They kill their prey in a special way called constriction. The snake wraps its

A Gaboon viper ready to strike.

Most zoo snakes are fed once a week. They're usually given dead rats and mice to eat. Sometimes zookeepers jiggle the food around to make the snakes want to catch it.

The big bulge in this African egg-eating snake's body is from an egg it has just swallowed.

body around the animal and squeezes until the animal stops breathing. Then the snake can take its time swallowing its catch.

Most snakes don't need to eat every day. The biggest pythons and boas may eat only a few large animals—such as pigs or deer—a year.

Poisonous snakes

Only about 400 kinds of snakes are poisonous. About half of these—including cobras, vipers, adders, and rattlesnakes—are dangerous to people. A poisonous snake uses its venom, or poison, to kill its prey before swallowing it.

The snake's poison is made in special glands in its head or body. The glands are linked to large, hollow teeth called fangs. When the snake bites, poison flows from its glands into its fangs and is injected into the prey.

This green mamba is about to seize its prey with its poisonous fangs.

A poisonous snake may also bite anything that attacks or disturbs it. Some cobras spit poison to warn off enemies.

A cobra spits venom to defend itself.

The Gaboon viper has the longest fangs of any poisonous snake.

When they're feeding poisonous snakes, zookeepers hold the food on long tongs so they won't get bitten.

Moving

It might seem like it would be difficult to move around without legs, but snakes are very good at it. The black mamba snake can move faster than a human can run.

Snakes have different ways of moving on the ground. Some move in a straight line by pushing against the ground with big scales on their body. Others move in "S"-shaped curves. They push at the points where their body bends.

A sidewinder adder slithers across sand dunes in the desert.

Snakes are easy to keep in zoos because they don't mind not being able to travel very far. They just need some rocks and branches to slither over.

A green tree python wraps its strong coils around a branch.

Most snakes can climb trees. Some, such as the green tree python, are extra good at climbing because they have a special grasping tail. The snake can use its tail to hold on to branches.

A paradise tree snake jumps from a branch and glides gently through the air to another tree.

Keeping safe

Most snakes, except for the very biggest, have enemies. Birds, mammals, and even other snakes will eat them. Many snakes try to stay safe by keeping out of sight. The colors of some snakes help them blend in with fallen leaves on the ground or twigs on trees.

A Gaboon viper lies among fallen leaves. Its color and pattern look like the leaves, making the snake hard to see.

A secretary bird catches a snake with its feet.

Each time a rattlesnake molts, another ring is added to its rattle.

The cobra scares off enemies by making itself look bigger. It has loose skin on each side of its head. When it's disturbed, the cobra spreads out this skin, making its head look more threatening.

The rattlesnake shakes the rattle at the end of its tail as a warning. The rattle is made of rings of hardened scales and makes a buzzing noise when shaken.

Eggs and young

Most snakes lay eggs. After laying them in hollows in the ground and covering them with earth and leaves to keep them warm, most snakes leave their eggs.

A few snakes, such as the Indian python, look after their eggs more carefully. The mother snake curls around her eggs and keeps them warm with her own body until they are ready to hatch.

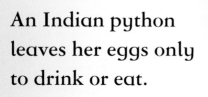

An Indian python leaves her eggs only to drink or eat.

When the young snakes hatch, they look like tiny adult snakes. Snakes don't live in families, so the young have to start taking care of themselves and finding their own food right away.

A baby snake has a special "egg tooth" to help it break out of its egg.

The mother snake has left these eggs to hatch on their own.

Zoo snakes are given nesting boxes where they can lay their eggs and cover them with straw. Sometimes eggs may be taken away and kept warm in an incubator, especially if the snake is a very rare kind.

Live young

Some snakes don't lay eggs. Instead, the mother keeps her eggs inside her body while they develop. The eggs don't have a proper shell but are covered by an outer skin called a membrane. When the young are ready to hatch, the eggs are pushed out of the mother's body. The young then break through the outer skin.

When young snakes are born live in the zoo, they are taken from their mother and put in their own enclosures right away.

The anaconda gives birth to its young in this way. The mother keeps about 20 to 40 young inside her as they grow. When the snakes hatch, they are about two feet (60 cm) long.

Both the anaconda (left) and the boa constrictor (right) keep their developing eggs inside their body.

23

Snake senses

Like other animals, snakes need to see, hear, and smell to get around and find food. Snakes don't have eyelids, so they can't blink. They can see movement well, but they probably can't see much else.

Snakes don't have ears on the outside of their body. But they can hear some sounds, and they can pick up the feeling of movements on the ground.

Sight is much more important than hearing for most snakes, including this black mamba.

A snake's sense of smell is very good. In addition to smelling with its nose, a snake flicks its forked tongue in and out to pick up smells from the air, water, or ground. This helps a snake track its prey and stay away from enemies.

The parrot snake hunts frogs in the jungles of South America.

A rhinoceros viper explores the world with its forked tongue.

Special senses

Many snakes can sense the heat given off by other animals. Some, such as rattlesnakes and pit vipers, have a special way of finding prey. These snakes have a deep pit on each side of their head between their nose and eyes.

This rattlesnake is about to catch a mouse it has tracked down by sensing its heat.

Pit vipers are named for the heat-sensing pit near their eyes.

The pits allow the snake to "see" the heat given off by animals such as rats and mice and to figure out where the animals are. In this way, the snake can track down its food even on the darkest night.

Snake fact file

Here is some more information about snakes. Your mom and dad might like to read this so you can talk about snakes some more when you see them at the zoo, or perhaps you can read these pages together.

Snakes

Snakes belong to a group of animals called reptiles. Other reptiles include lizards, turtles, and crocodiles. Some of the main types of snakes are boas, pythons, king snakes, garter snakes, rattlesnakes, mambas, cobras, and vipers.

Where snakes live

Snakes live in most parts of the world, but there are more snakes in tropical countries than anywhere else. There are no snakes in Antarctica, New Zealand, Iceland, Greenland, or Ireland.

Snake numbers

There are plenty of most kinds of snakes, but there are at least 70 different types that are rare or becoming rare. There are two main reasons for this. First, some of the places where snakes live, such as tropical forests, are being destroyed. Second, many snakes are being caught and sold as pets or killed for their skin.

Size

One of the smallest snakes is the Brahminy blind snake, which is only a couple of inches (5 cm) long and weighs a fraction of an ounce. Many thread snakes are also only a few inches (7.5 cm) long. The biggest snakes are the anaconda and the reticulated python. The anaconda lives in South American jungles and can be up to 33 feet (10 m) long, although not all anacondas reach this size. It can weigh up to 330 pounds (150 kg). The reticulated python, which lives in Asia, is also about 33 feet (10 m) long but is not as heavy as the anaconda.

Find out more

If you want to learn more about snakes, check out these Web sites:

Smithsonian National Zoological Park: Snakes
http://nationalzoo.si.edu/Animals/ReptilesAmphibians/Herps.cfm?type=snake

San Diego Zoo: Reptiles
http://www.sandiegozoo.org/animalbytes/a-reptiles.html

Indianapolis Zoo: Snakes
http://www.indyzoo.com/content.aspx?cid=436

Glossary

Enclosure
The area where an animal lives in a zoo.

Gland
A part of the body that makes a special substance, such as poison in snakes.

Incubator
A machine for keeping eggs warm until they hatch.

Prey
An animal that is hunted and eaten by another animal.

Reptile
A cold-blooded animal that has a backbone.

Scales

Hard pieces of skin that cover a reptile's body.

Skeleton

The bony framework of the body.

Tropical

The parts of the world around the equator where it is always hot.

Index

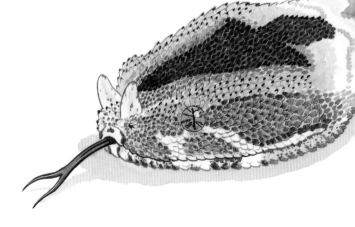